HAL•LEONARD
HARMONICA
PLAY•ALONG

POP ROCK

T0066108

Harmonica by Clint Hoover & Jim Liban

ISBN 978-1-4234-2312-6

Visit Hal Leonard Online at
www.halleonard.com

HAL•LEONARD®
CORPORATION
7777 W. BLUEMOUND RD. P.O. BOX 13819
MILWAUKEE, WISCONSIN 53213

HAL•LEONARD

HARMONICA PLAY·ALONG

POP ROCK

VOL. 1

CONTENTS

And When I Die

Words and Music by Laura Nyro

HARMONICA
Player: Steve Katz
Harp Key: D Diatonic

Intro
Free time

Throat vibrato throughout.

Moderately ♩ = 138

Verse

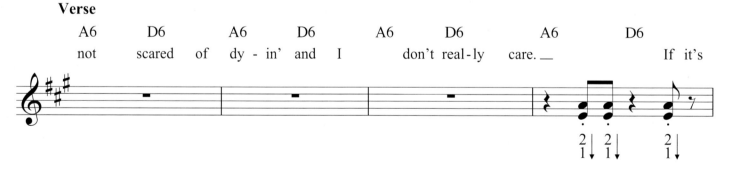

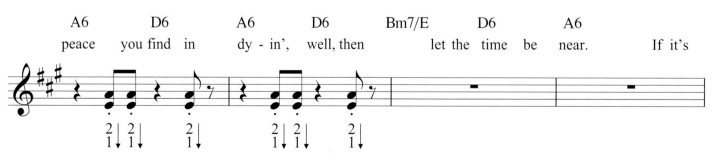

𝄋

Faster ♩ = 113

G				D			G	D
peace	you	find	in	dy - in'	and __		if	dy - in'	time	is

(2.) *See additional lyrics*

E7sus4		Bm7	C#m7	D	D/E	A	D
near, __	just	bun - dle	up __ my	cof - fin	'cause it's		cold way down

accel.

A	D	A	D	A
there.	I hear __	that it's	cold way down	there.	Yeah. __

Fast ♩ = 128

Dmaj7	C#m7	Bm7	D/E	A	D	A	D	A
Cra -	zy	cold	way down	there. __			And when I

Chorus

Bm7	C#m7	F#m7	A7
die _____	and when I'm	gone, __	there'll be

To Coda ⊕

Dmaj7	C#m7	Bm7 D/E
one	child born	in this world to car - ry on, to car - ry

5

Interlude

Piano Solo

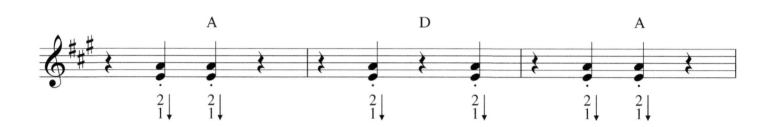

Interlude
Slower ♩ = 138

2. Now

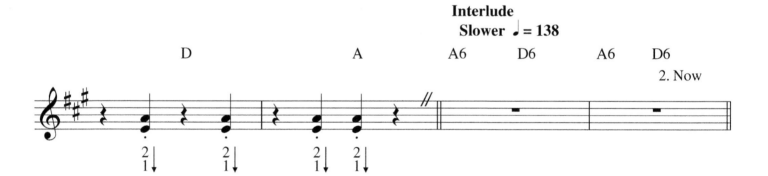

Verse

| A6 | D6 | A6 | D6 | A6 | D6 | A6 | D6 |

trou - bles are man-y. They're as   deep as a well. __   I can

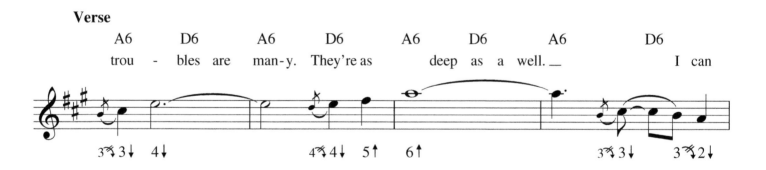

D.S. al Coda

| A6 | D6 | A6 | D6 | A6 | D6 | A6 |

swear there ain't no heav-en but I pray there ain't no hell.

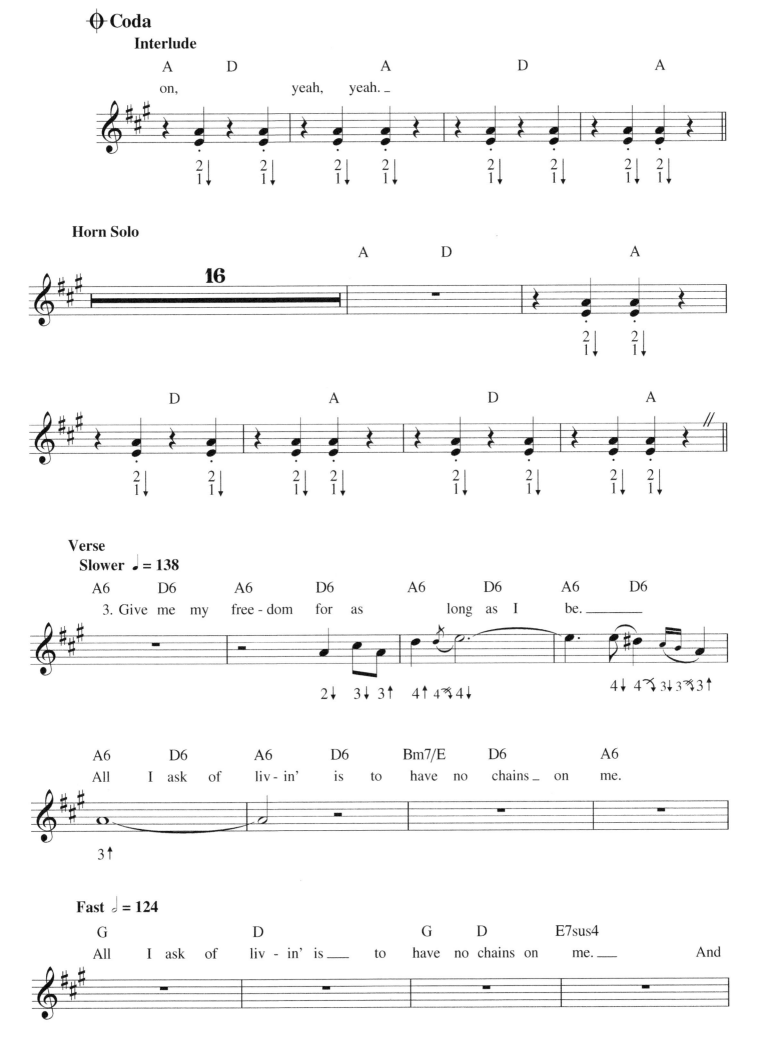

accel.

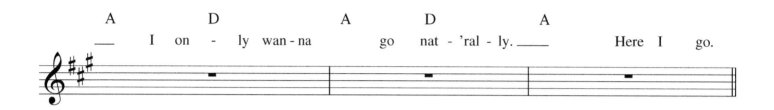

Outro

w/ Lead Voc. ad lib. (next 16 meas.)

Additional Lyrics

(2.) Swear there ain't no heaven
And I pray there ain't no hell.
But I'll never know by living,
Only my dyin' will tell.
Yes, only my dyin' will tell.
Yeah, only my dyin' will tell.

Bright Side of the Road

Words and Music by Van Morrison

H A R M O N I C A

Player: Van Morrison
Harp Key: F Diatonic

Intro
Moderately fast ♩ = 178 (♫ = ♩♪)

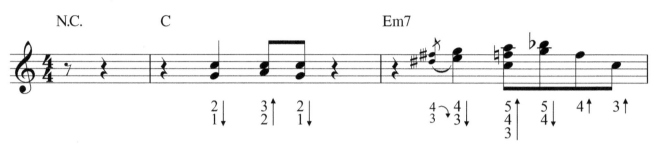

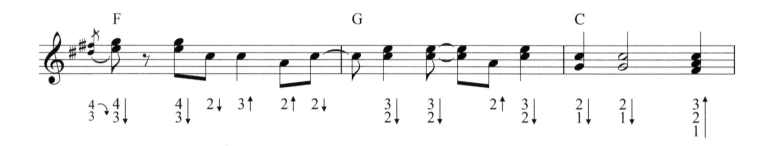

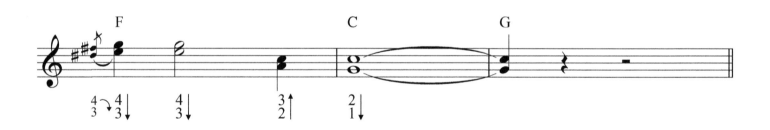

Verse

1. From the dark ___ end ___ of ___ the street ___
2. *See additional lyrics*

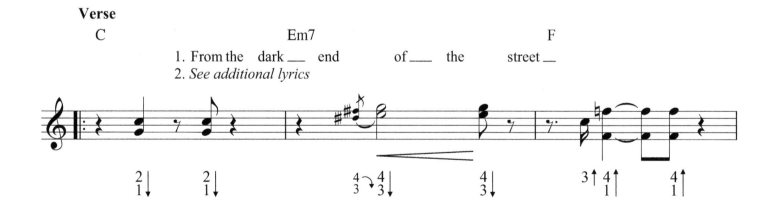

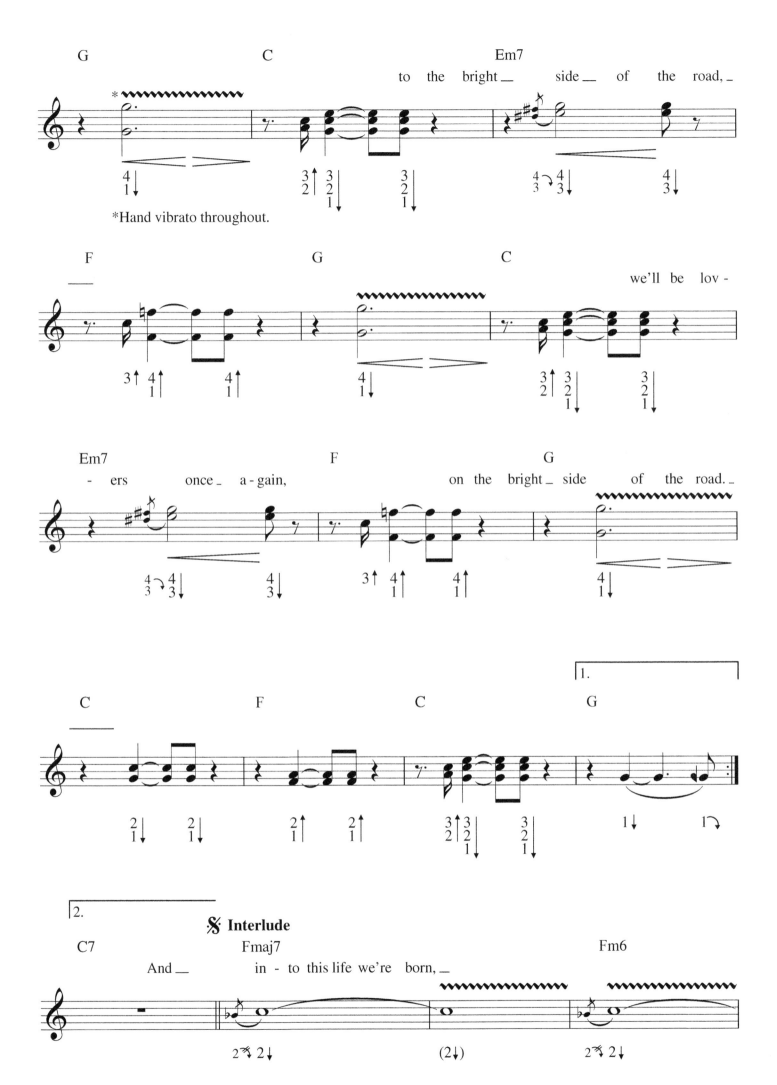

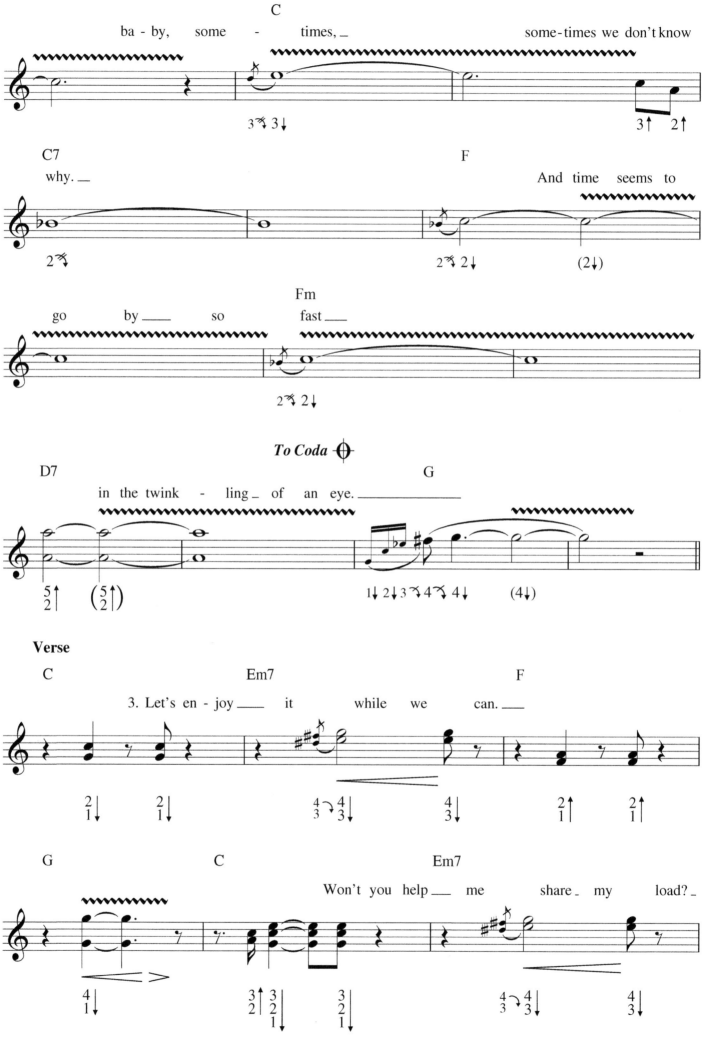

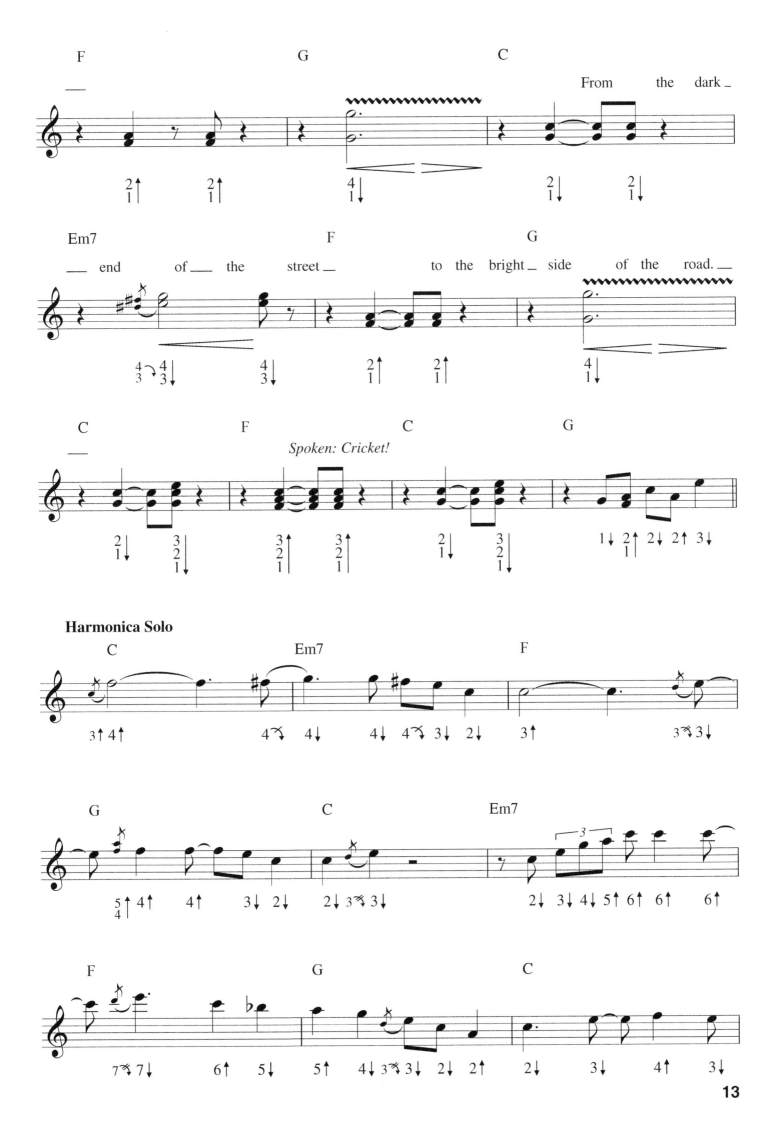

D.S. al Coda

And —

✛ Coda

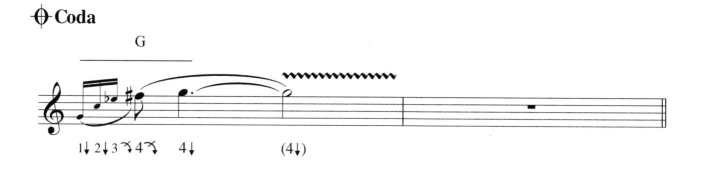

Verse

4. Let's en - joy   it   while — we   can. —
5., 6. *See additional lyrics*

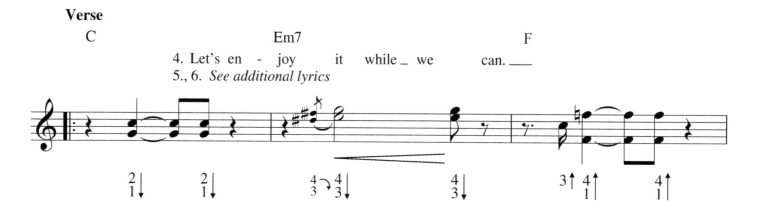

Help — me   sing — my   song. —

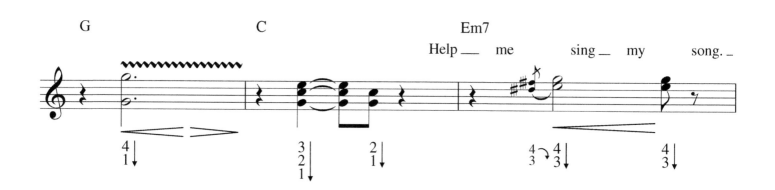

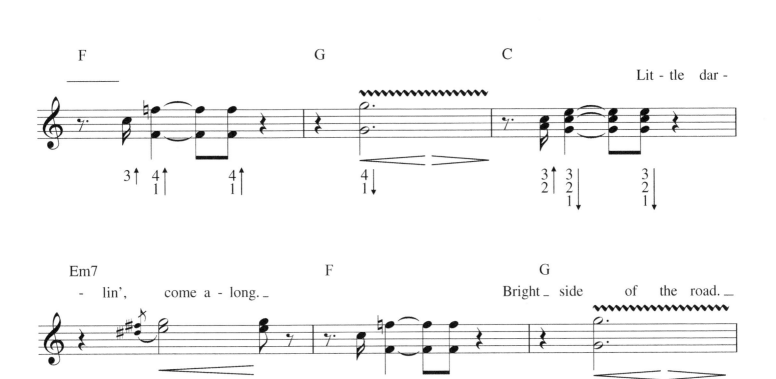

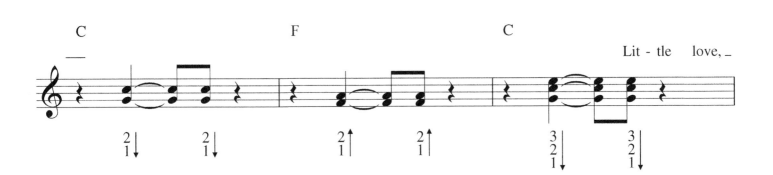

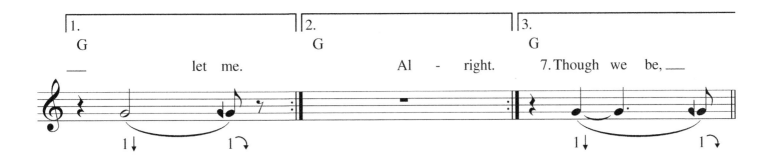

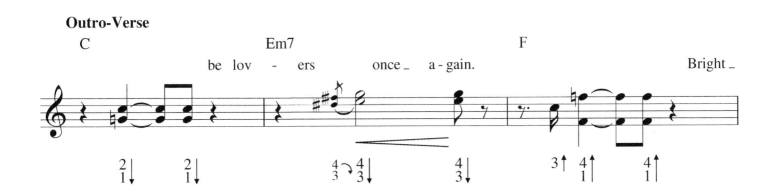

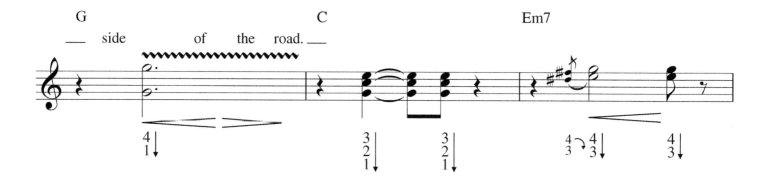

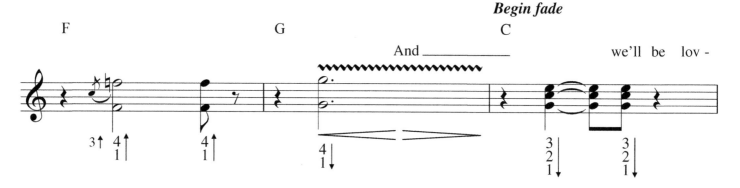

Begin fade

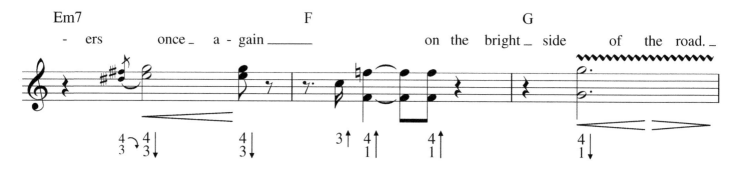

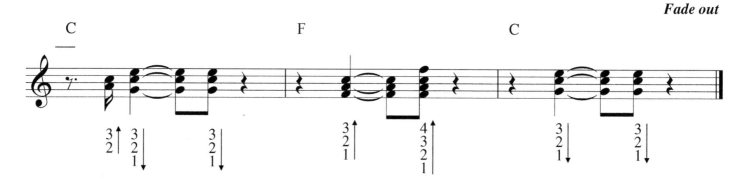

Fade out

Additional Lyrics

2. Little darlin', come with me.
   Won't you help me share my load?
   From the dark end of the street
   To the bright side of the road.

5. From the dark end of the street
   To the bright side of the road,
   Little darlin', come along
   To the bright side of the road.

6. From the dark end of the street,
   Oh, babe, to the bright side of the road,
   We'll be lovers once again,
   On the bright side of the road.

I Should Have Known Better

Words and Music by John Lennon and Paul McCartney

HARMONICA
Player: John Lennon
Harp Key: C Diatonic

Intro
Moderately ♩ = 132

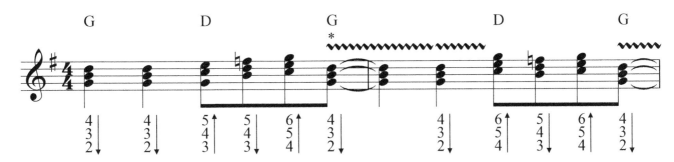

*Warble vibrato throughout

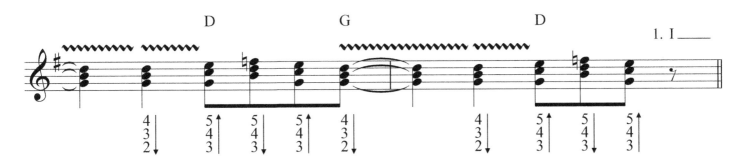

1. I ____

Verse

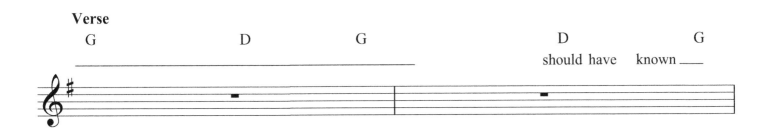

should have known ____

bet - ter with a girl like you.

That I would

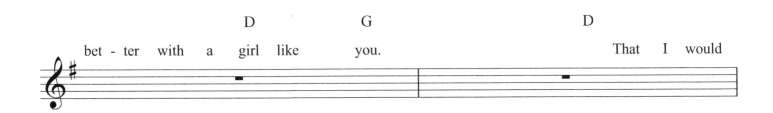

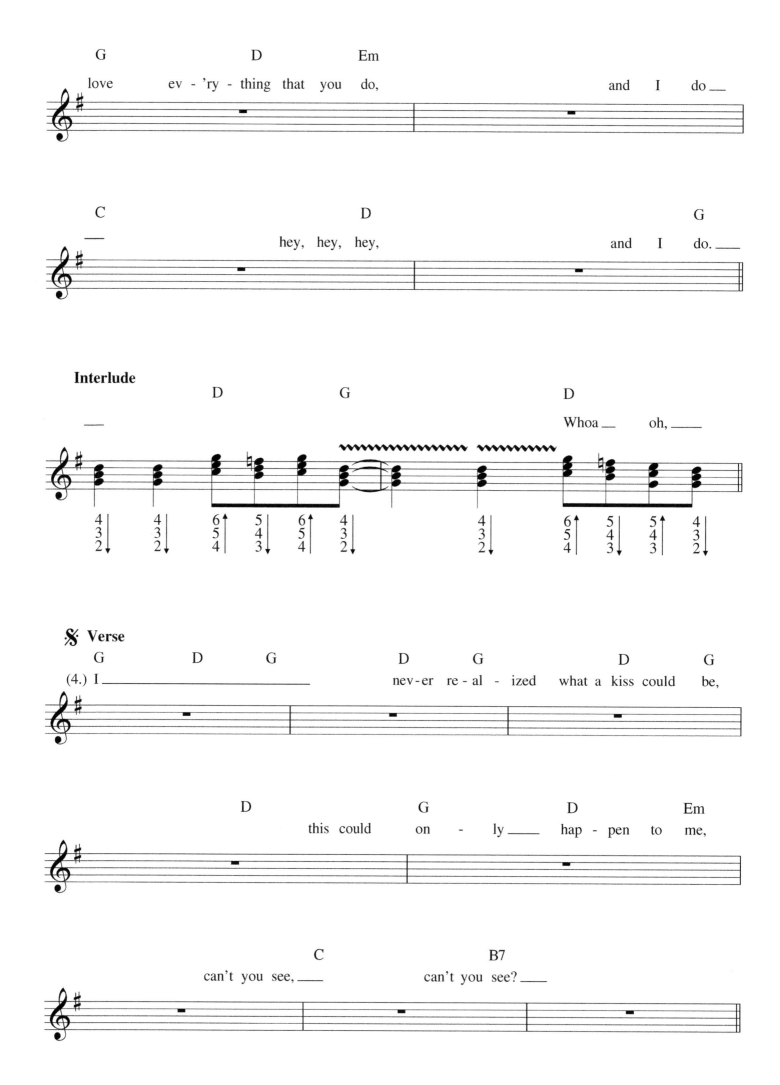

18

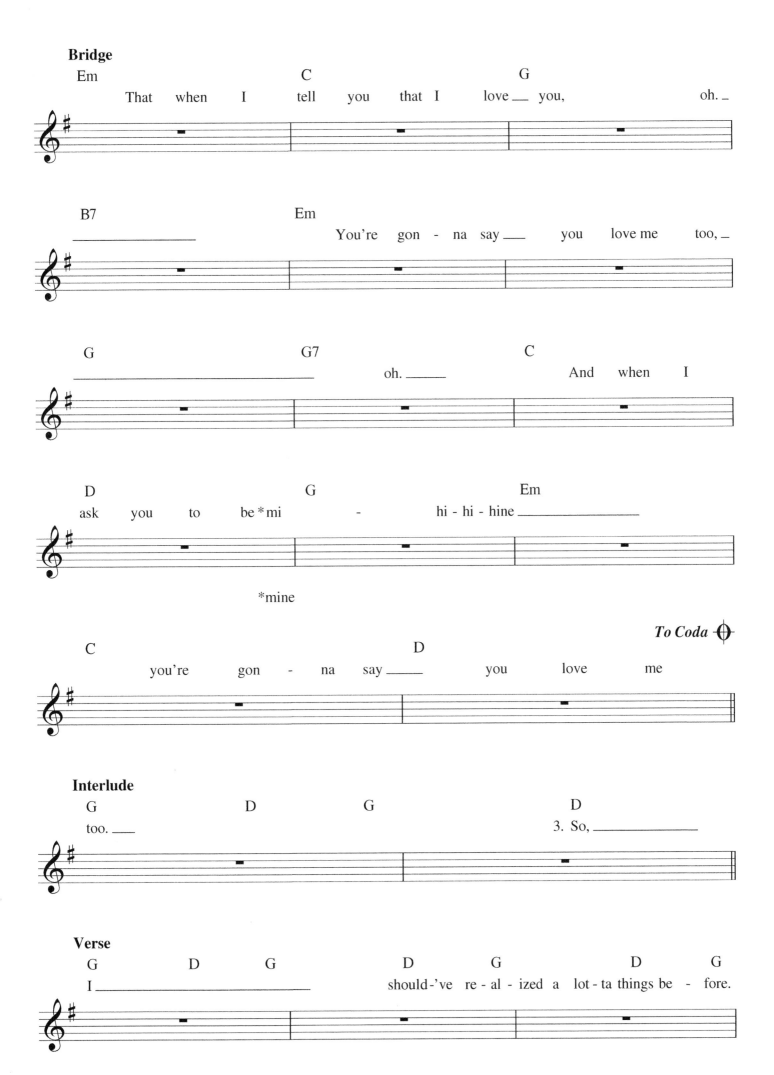

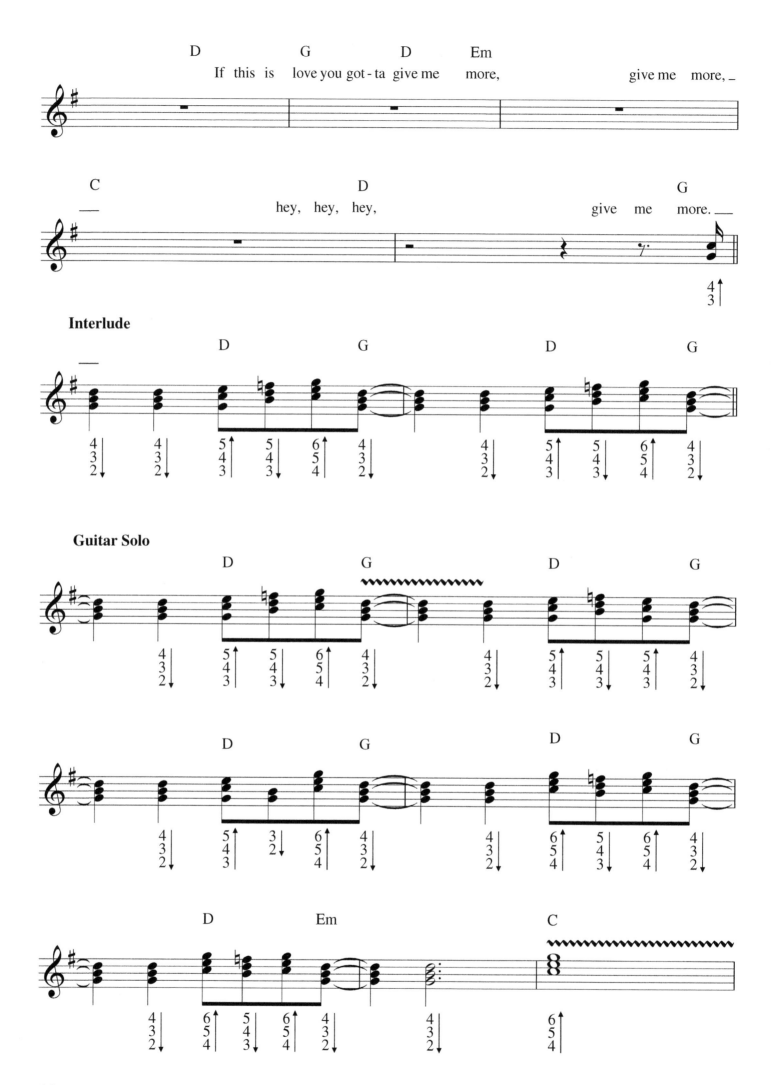

Interlude

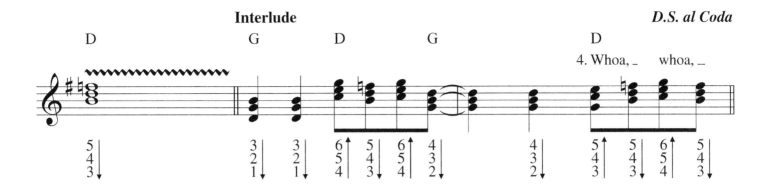

Coda

Outro

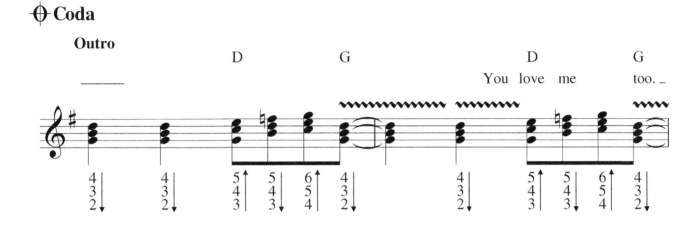

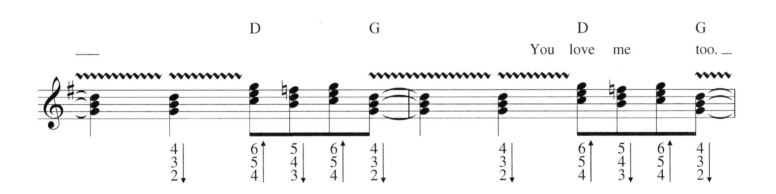

Begin fade   *Fade out*

Living in the U.S.A.

Words and Music by Steve Miller

H A R M O N I C A

Player: Steve Miller
Harp Key: D Diatonic

Intro

Moderately fast ♩ = 175

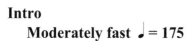

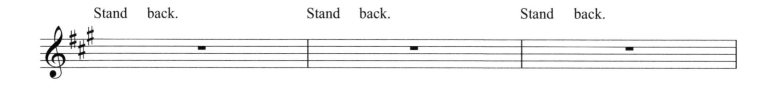

*Throat vibrato throughout.

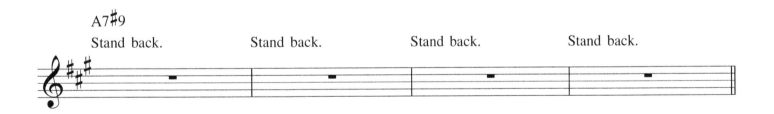

A7#9

Stand back.   Stand back.   Stand back.   Stand back.

N.C. (Am7)

Chorus

(A7)　　　　　　　　　　　　　　　　Am

Doo,　doo, doo, doo, doo,　　doo, ____ doo, ____

3↓　4↑　　4↷　4↓　1↓　1↓　1↓　2↑　2↑　2↷　2↷

liv - in' in the U. S.　A. ____　　　　　　Doo,　doo, doo, doo, doo,　　doo, _

1↓　1↓　1↓　1↓　2↑　2↑　2↷　　　　1↓　1↓　1↓　2↑　2↑　2↷

____ doo, ____　　　liv - in' in the U. S.　A. ____

2↷　　　　1↓　　　1↓　2↑　2↑　2↷

Verse

Am7　　　　　　　　　　　　　　　　Bm7　　Am7

1. Where are you go - in'　to? ____　　　What are you gon-na do? _

2↷　　　2↷ 2↷ 2↑　1↓

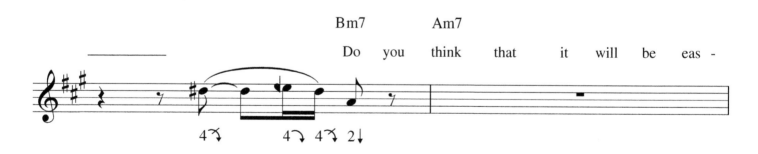

Bm7　　Am7

Do　you　think　that　it　will　be　eas -

4↷　　　4↷　4↷ 2↓

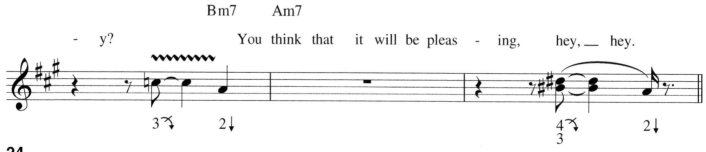

Bm7　　Am7

- y?　　You think that　it will be pleas - ing,　hey, _ hey.

3↷　　2↓　　　　　　　　　　　4↷　　　2↓
　　　　　　　　　　　　　　　　　　　3

Interlude

A7#9

(Stand back.) And what'd you say? _ (Stand back.) I _ won't pay. _ (Stand back.) I'd rath-er play.

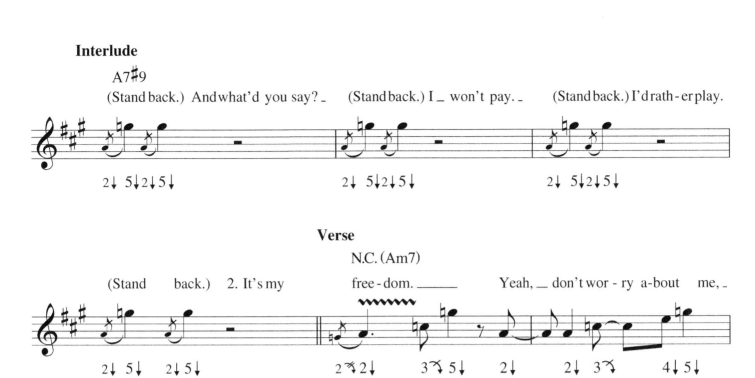

2↓ 5↓2↓5↓   2↓ 5↓2↓5↓   2↓ 5↓2↓5↓

Verse

N.C. (Am7)

(Stand   back.) 2. It's my   free - dom. _____   Yeah, _ don't wor - ry a-bout   me, _

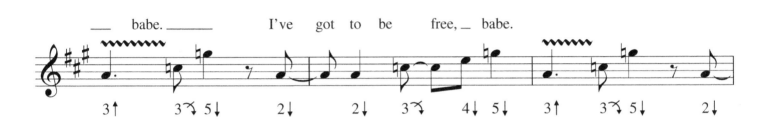

2↓ 5↓ 2↓5↓   2↗2↓ 3↗ 5↓ 2↓   2↓ 3↗   4↓5↓

__ babe. _____   I've   got   to   be   free, _ babe.

3↑   3↗ 5↓   2↓   2↓   3↗   4↓ 5↓   3↑   3↗ 5↓   2↓

(A7)

Hey,   hey, _ hey, _____   yeah. _

2↓   3↗   4↓ 5↓   3↑   3↗5↓   2↓   3↓ 4↑   4↗ 4↓

Chorus

Am   Bm7   Am

Doo, doo, doo, doo, doo,   doo, __ doo, _____   liv - in' in the U. S. A. _

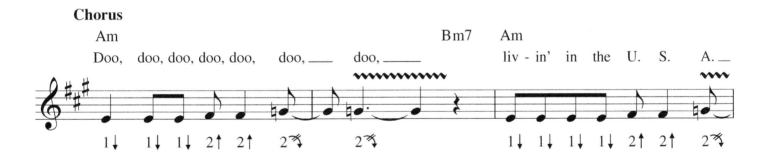

1↓   1↓ 1↓ 2↑ 2↑   2↗   2↗   1↓ 1↓ 1↓ 1↓ 2↑ 2↑   2↗

Bm7   Am   Bm7

Doo, doo, doo, doo, doo,   doo, __ doo, _____

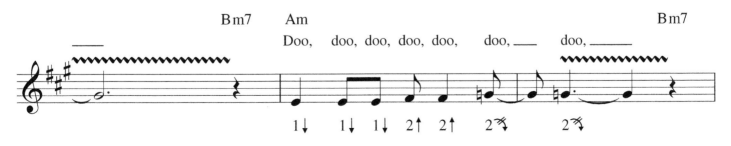

1↓   1↓ 1↓ 2↑ 2↑   2↗   2↗

25

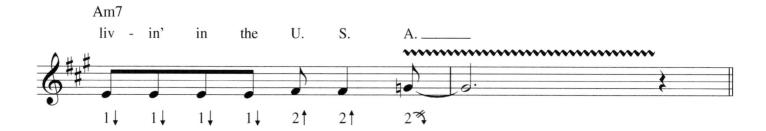

Interlude

Verse

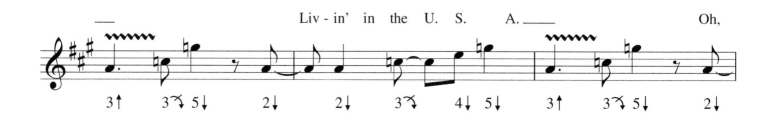

Interlude

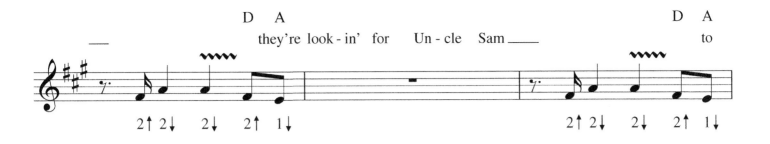

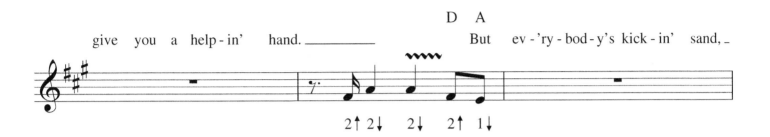

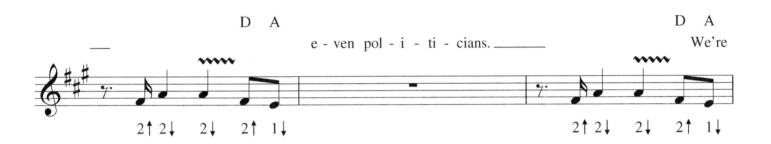

Bridge

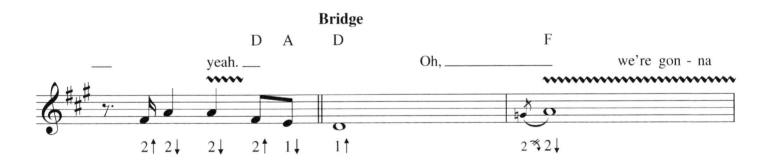

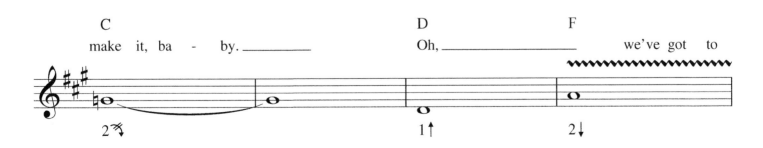

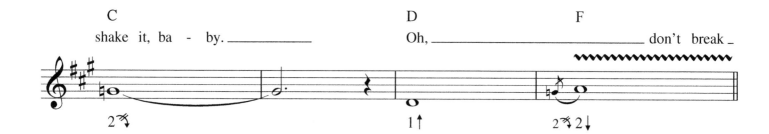

Interlude

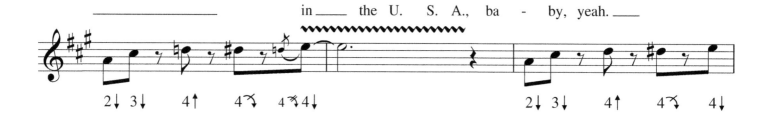

Outro-Chorus

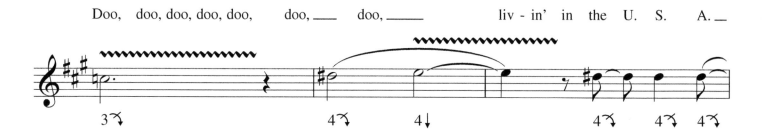

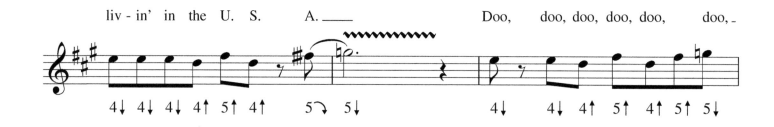

Piano Man

Words and Music by Billy Joel

HARMONICA

Player: Billy Joel
Harp Key: C Diatonic

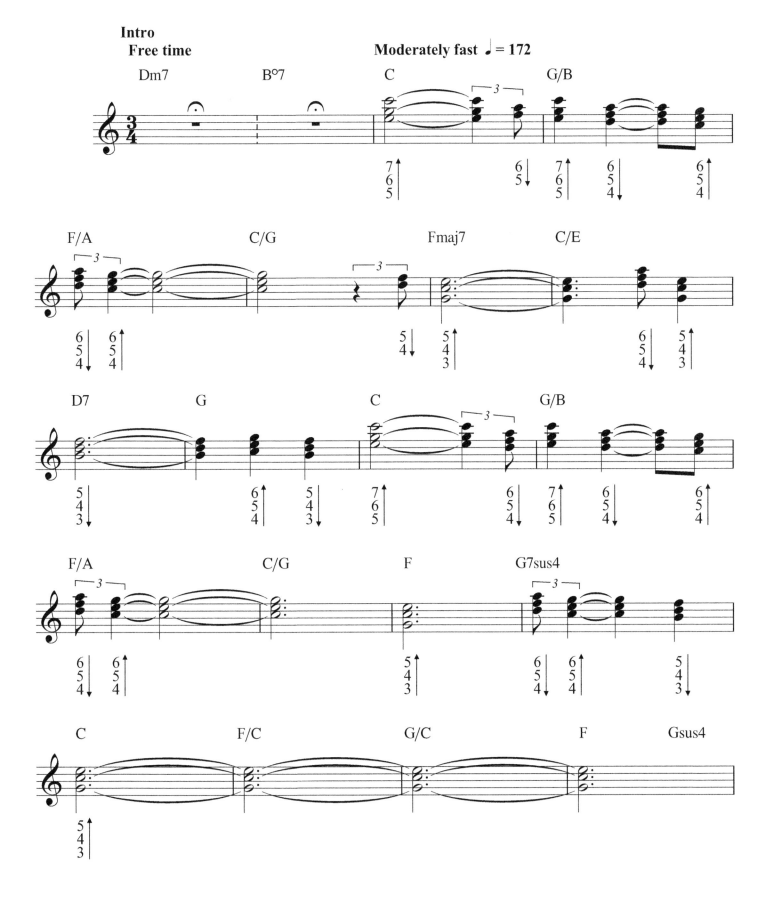

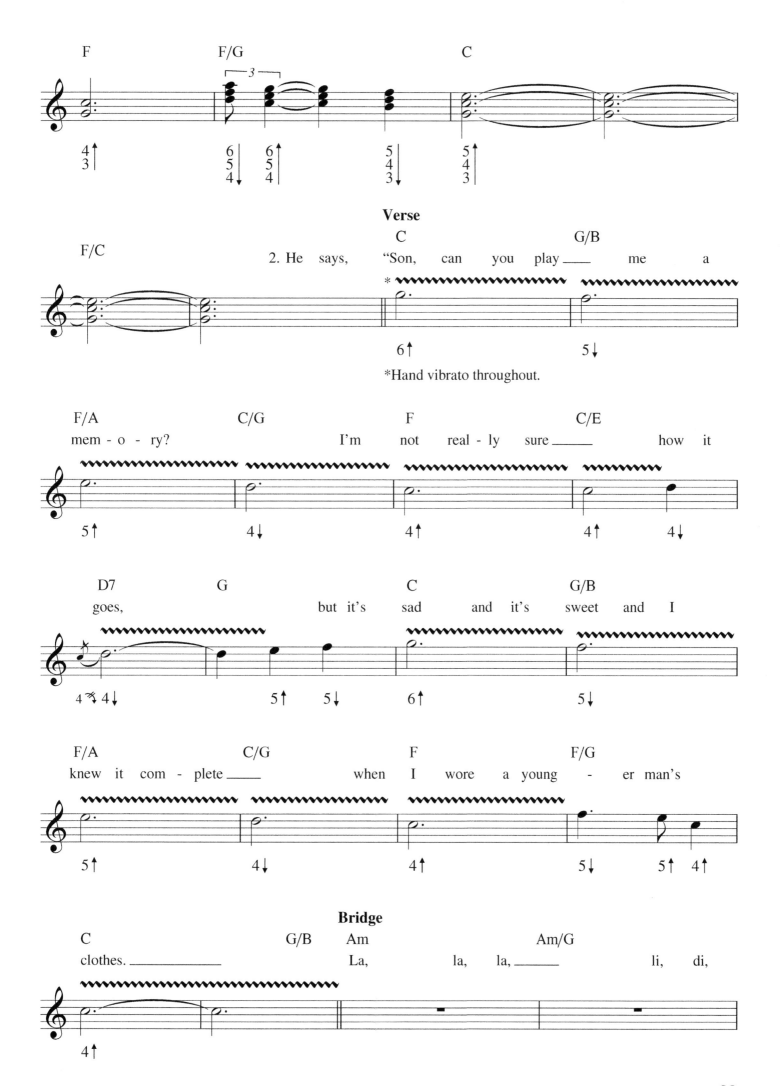

Verse

*Hand vibrato throughout.

Bridge

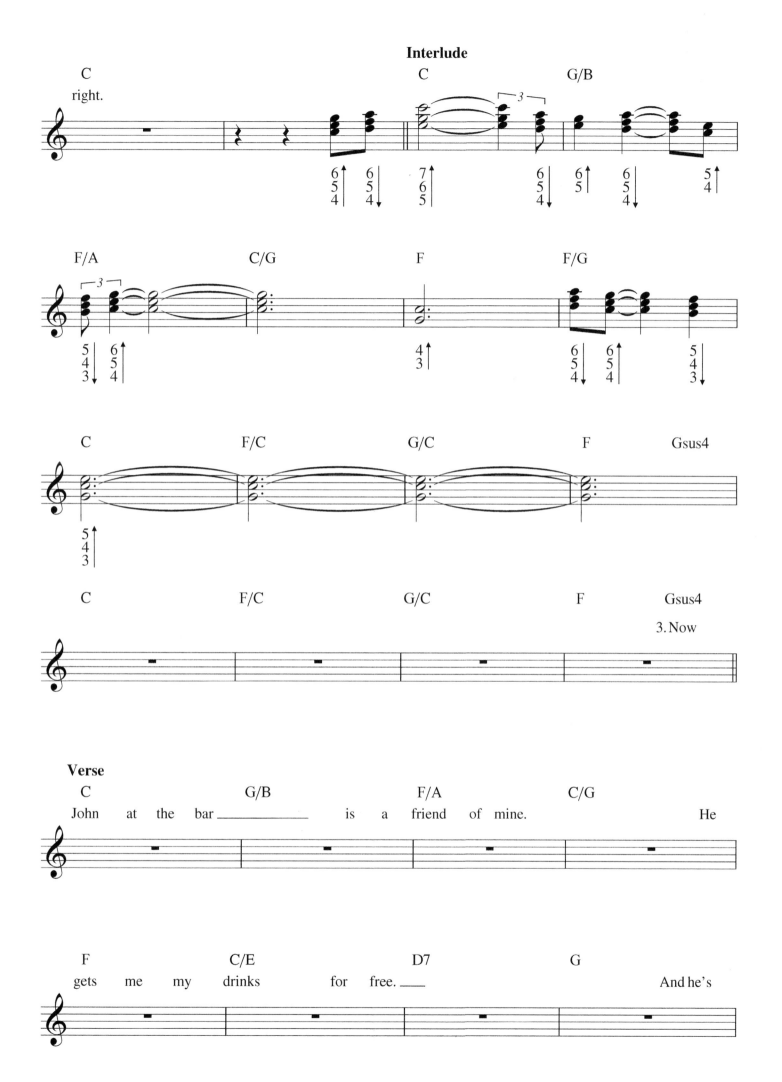

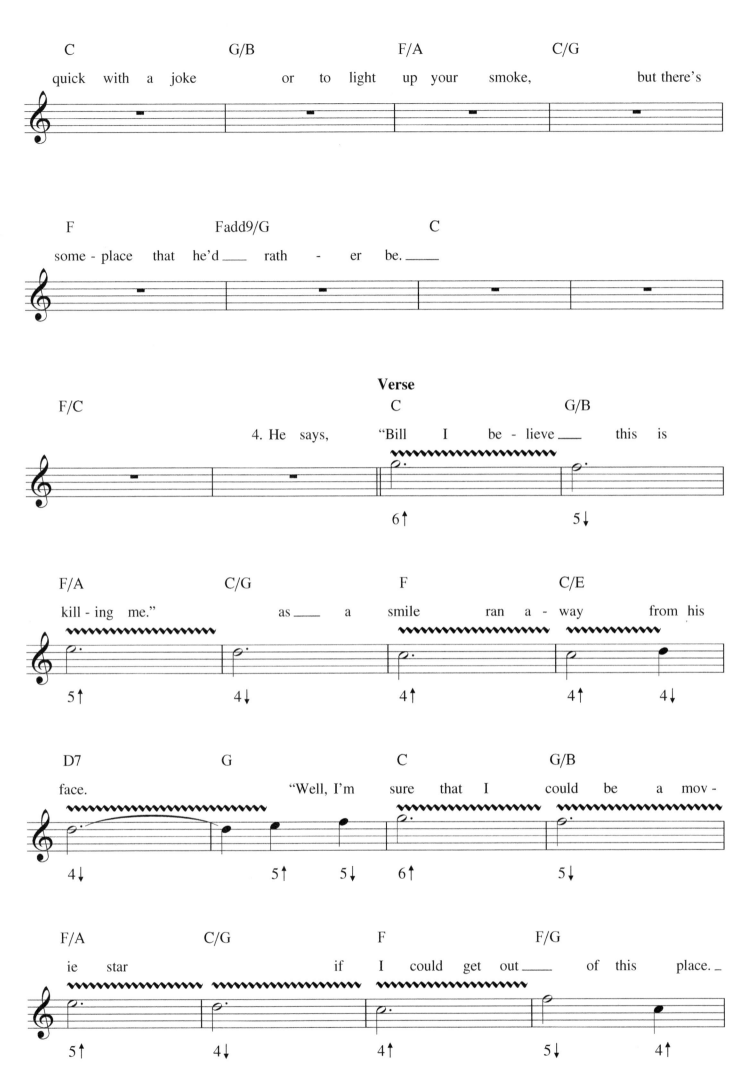

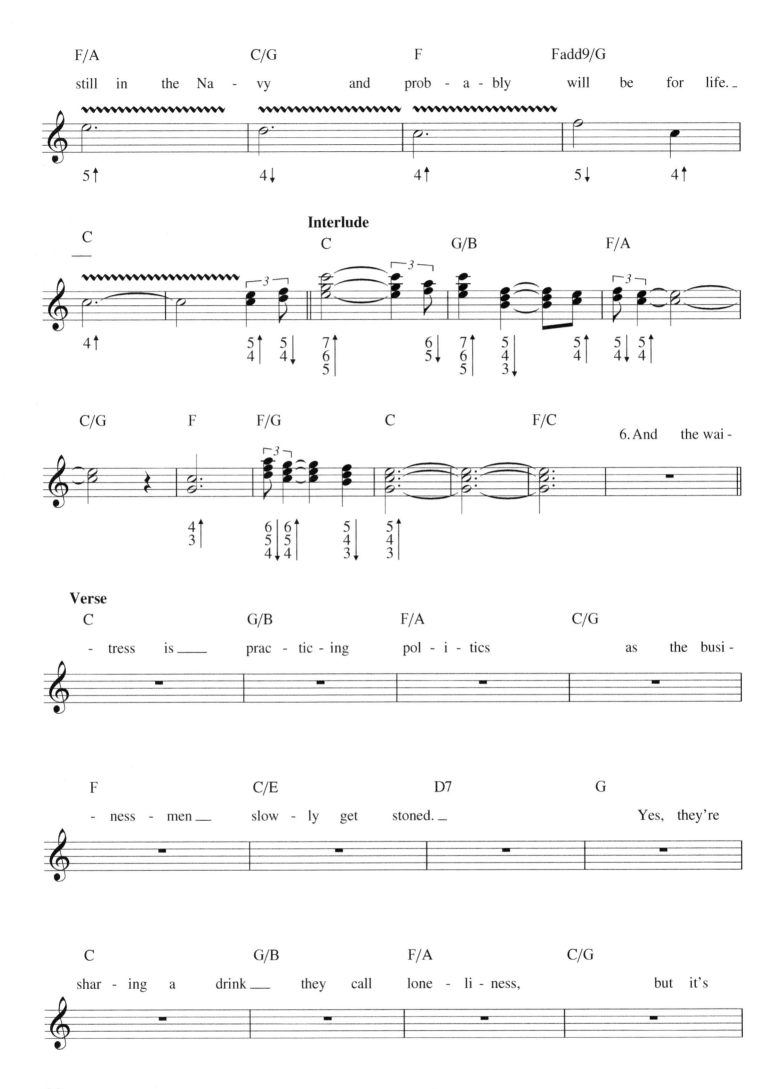

F   Fadd9/G   C

bet - ter   than   drink - in'   a - lone. ___

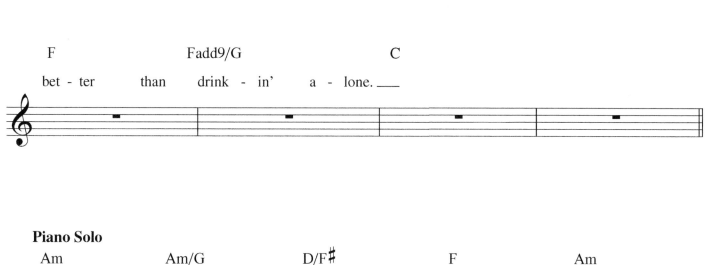

Piano Solo

Am   Am/G   D/F#   F   Am

Am/G   D/F#   F   Am   Am/G   D

G   G/F   C/E   G7/D

Chorus

C   G/B   F/A   C/G

Sing   us   a   song, __   you're the   pia - no   man. _

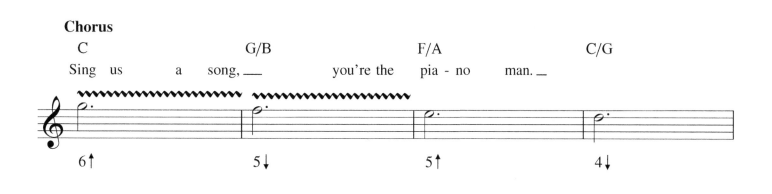

6↑   5↓   5↑   4↓

F   C/E   D7   G

Sing   us   a   song ____   to - night. __   Well, we're

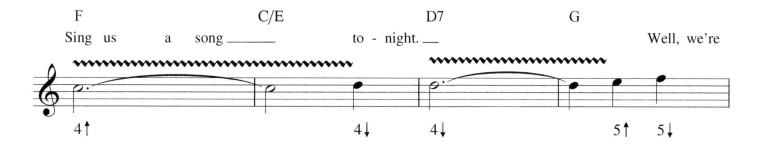

4↑   4↓   4↓   5↑   5↓

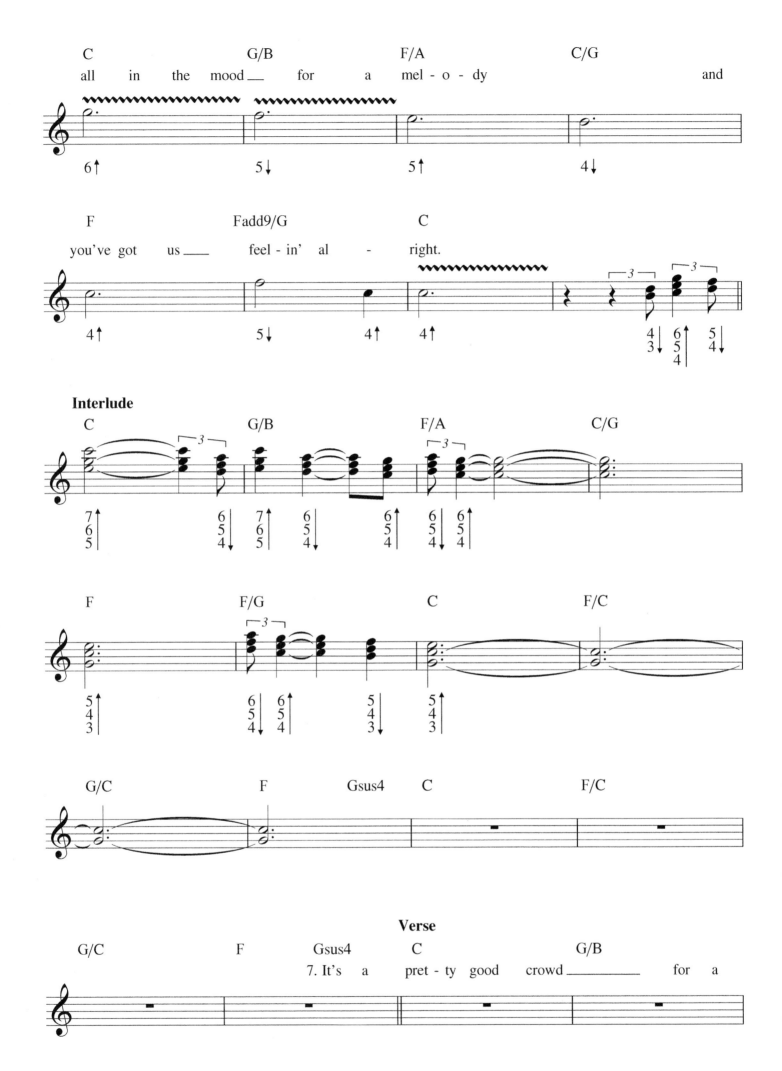

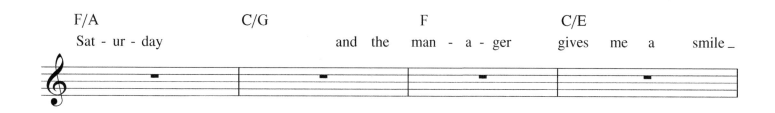

F/A   C/G   F   C/E

Sat - ur - day   and the man - a - ger   gives me a smile _

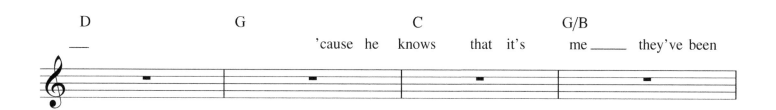

D   G   C   G/B

—   'cause he knows that it's me ____ they've been

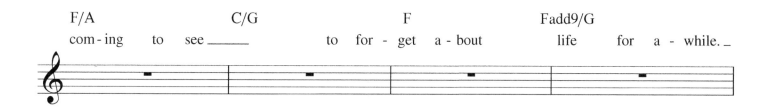

F/A   C/G   F   Fadd9/G

com - ing to see ____ to for - get a - bout life for a - while. _

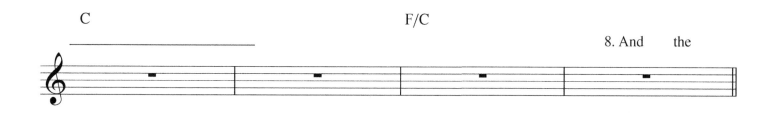

C   F/C

8. And the

Verse

C   G/B   F/A   C/G

pia - no, it sounds like a car - ni - val   and the mi -

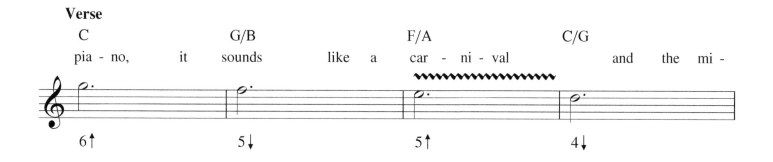

6↑   5↓   5↑   4↓

F   C/E   D7   G

- cro - phone smells like a beer   and they

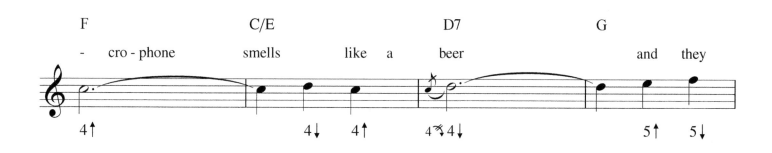

4↑   4↓   4↑   4↗4↓   5↑   5↓

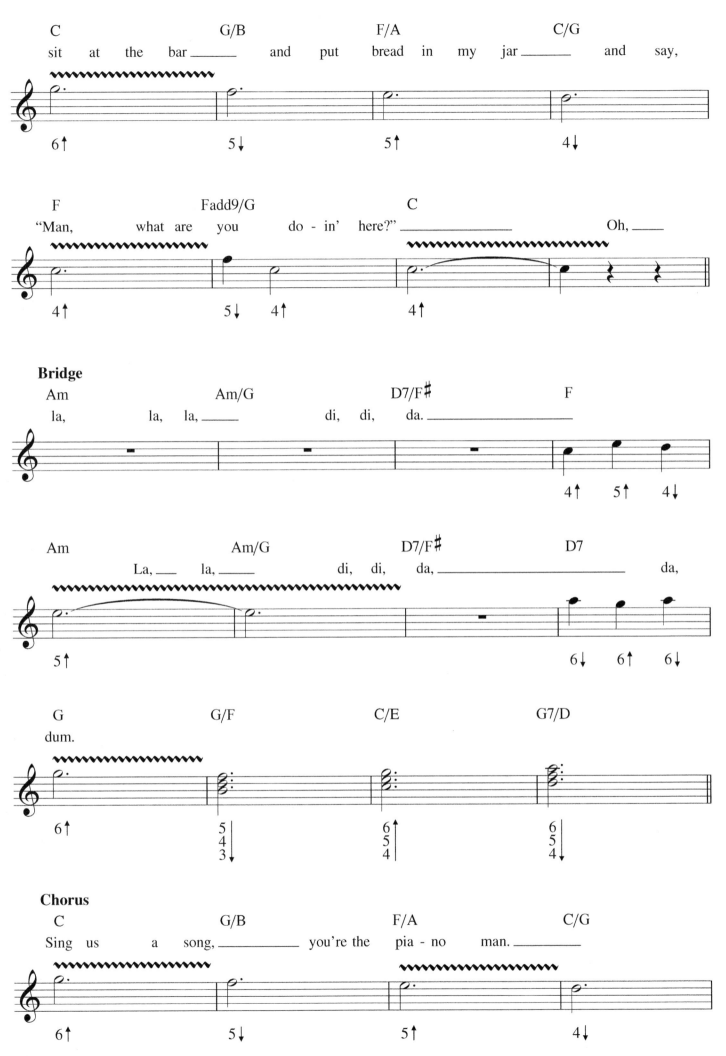

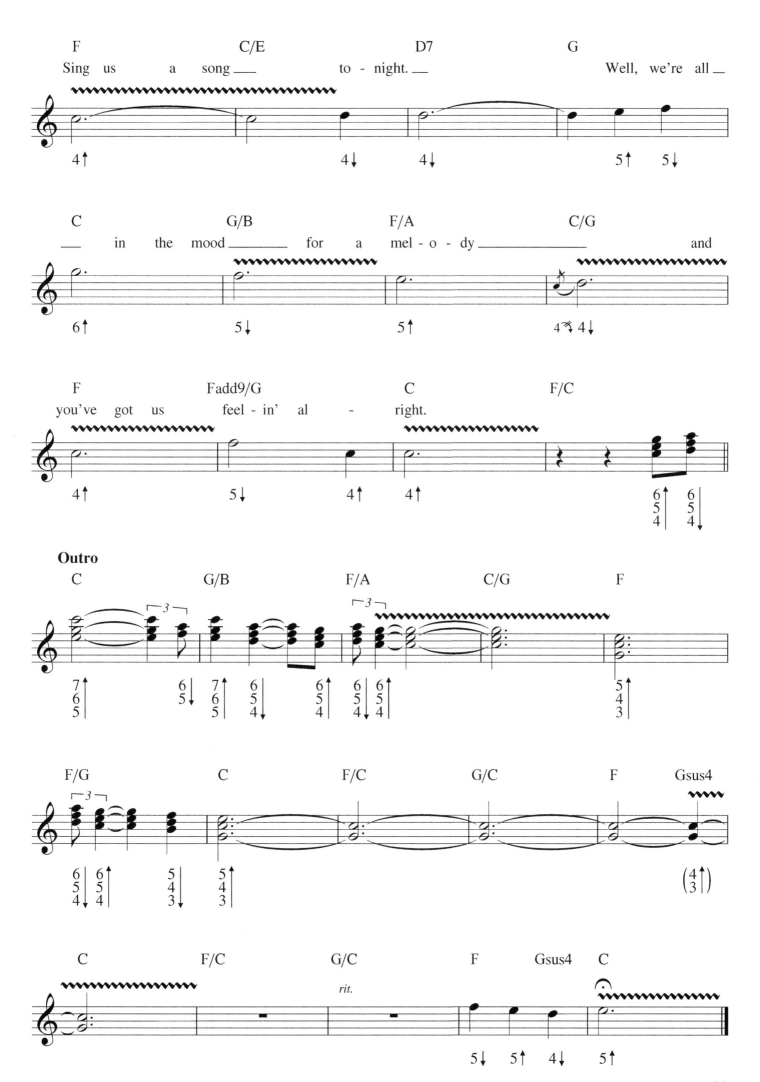

Outro

Low Rider

**Words and Music by Sylvester Allen, Harold R. Brown,
Morris Dickerson, Jerry Goldstein, Leroy Jordan,
Lee Oskar, Charles W. Miller and Howard Scott**

HARMONICA
Player: Lee Oskar
Harp Key: C Diatonic

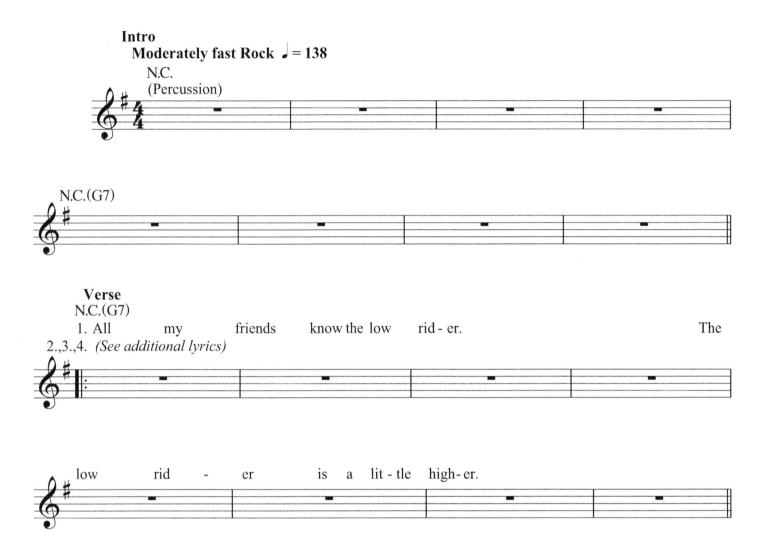

Outro

N.C.(G7)

Play 4 times Take a lit - tle trip, take a lit - tle trip,

take a lit - tle trip and see. _____ Take a lit - tle trip,

take a lit - tle trip, take a lit - tle trip with me. _____

Outro

2nd time, Harm. tacet

N.C.(G7)

Repeat and fade

Additional Lyrics

2. Low rider drives a little slower.
   Low rider, he's a real goer.

3. Low rider knows ev'ry street, yeah.
   Low rider is the one to meet, yeah.

4. Low rider don't use no gas now.
   Low rider don't drive too fast.

Miss You

Words and Music by Mick Jagger and Keith Richards

H A R M O N I C A
Player: Sugar Blue
Harp Key: D Diatonic

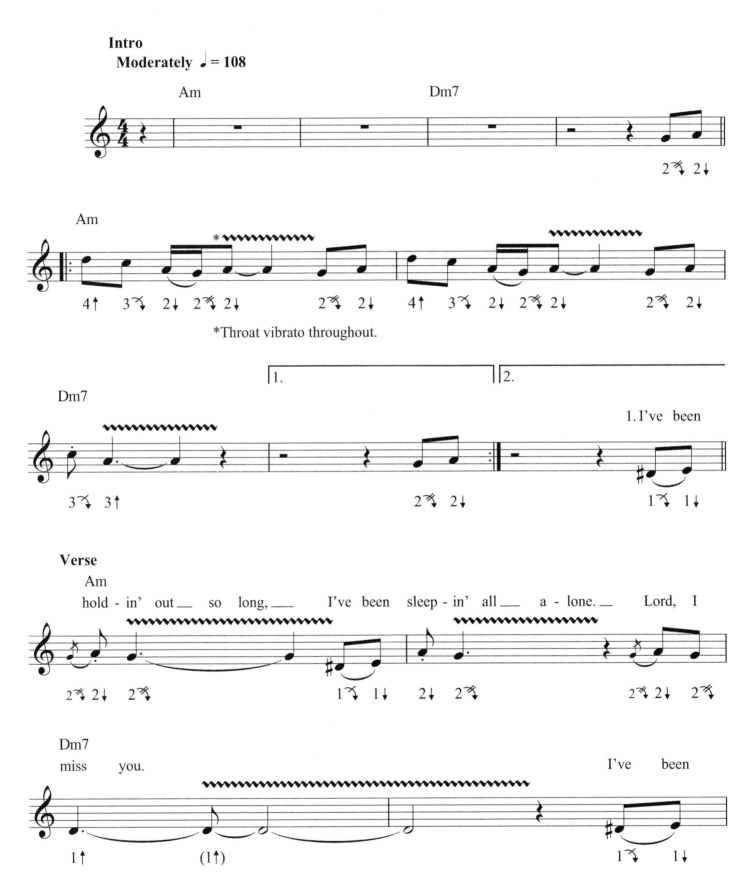

*Throat vibrato throughout.

Am

hang - in' on ___ the phone, ___ I've been sleep - in' all ___ a - lone. I wan-na

2↓ 2↗ 1↘ 1↓ 2↗ 2↓ 2↗ 2↗ 2↓ 2↗

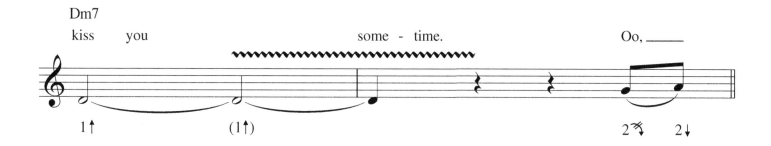

Dm7

kiss you some - time. Oo, ___

1↑ (1↑) 2↗ 2↓

Chorus

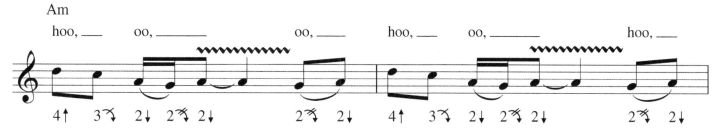

Am

hoo, ___ oo, ___ oo, ___ hoo, ___ oo, ___ hoo, ___

4↑ 3↗ 2↓ 2↗ 2↓ 2↗ 2↓ 4↑ 3↗ 2↓ 2↗ 2↓ 2↗ 2↓

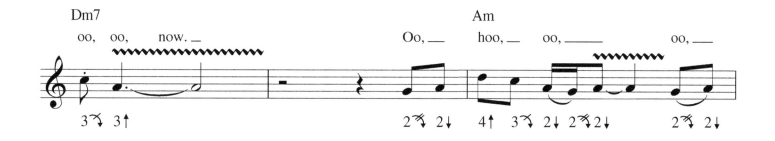

Dm7   Am

oo, oo, now. ___ Oo, ___ hoo, ___ oo, ___ oo, ___

3↗ 3↑ 2↗ 2↓ 4↑ 3↗ 2↓ 2↗ 2↓ 2↗ 2↓

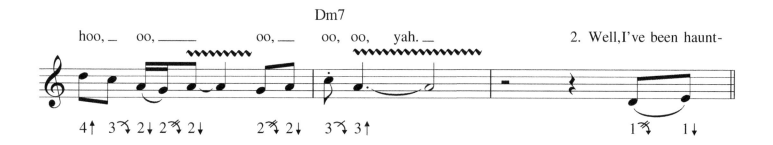

                 Dm7

hoo, ___ oo, ___ oo, ___ oo, oo, yah. ___ 2. Well, I've been haunt-

4↑ 3↗ 2↓ 2↗ 2↓ 2↗ 2↓ 3↗ 3↑ 1↗ 1↓

Verse

Am

- ed in ___ my sleep, you been star - rin' in ___ my dreams. ___ Lord, I

2↓ 2↗ 1↗ 1↓ 2↓ 2↗ 2↗ 2↓ 2↗

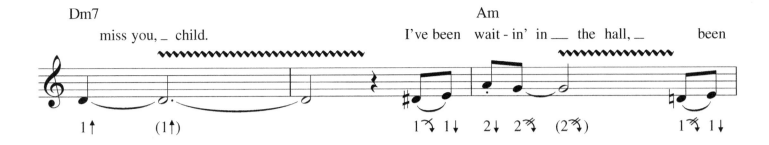

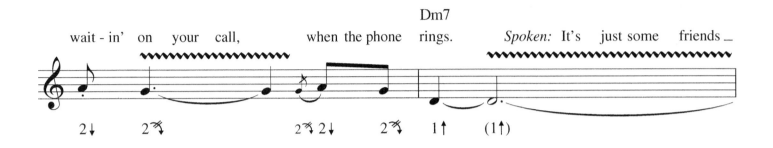

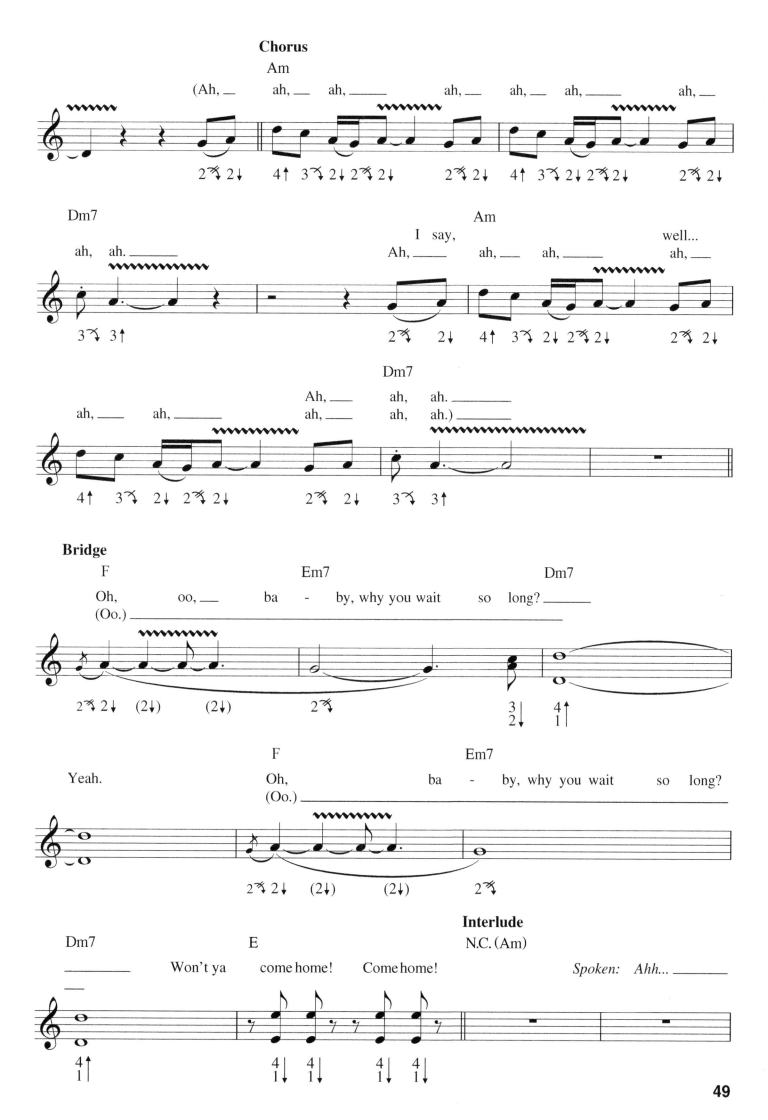

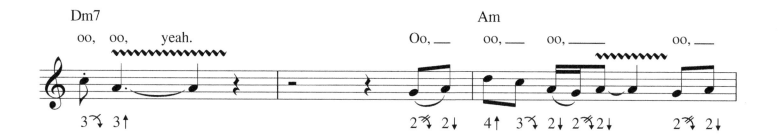

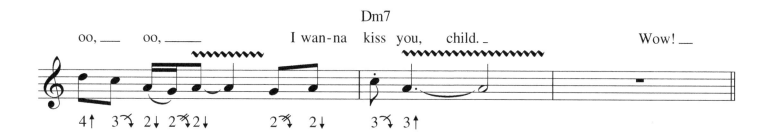

Saxophone Solo

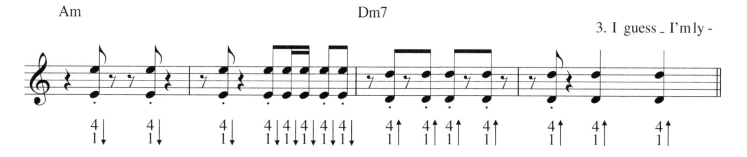

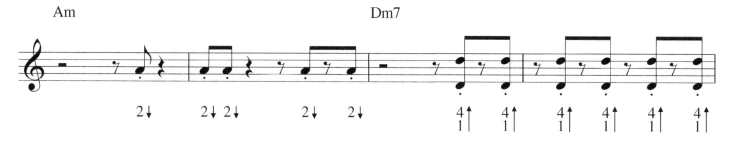

Verse

Chorus

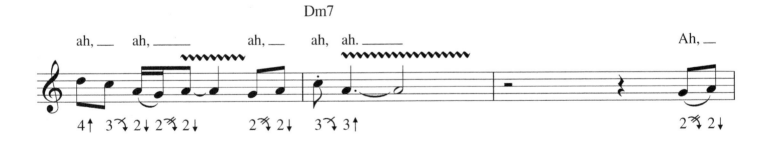

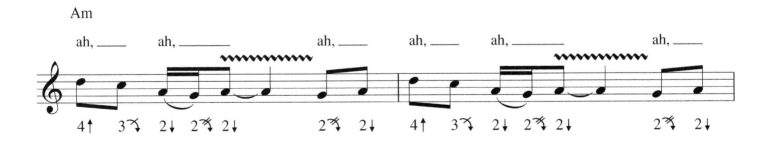

Dm7

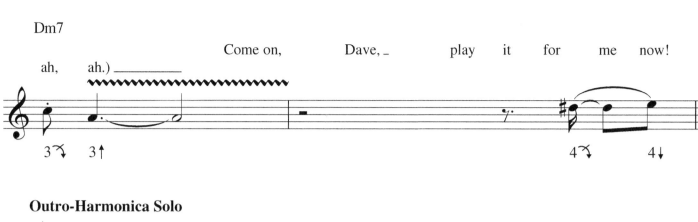

ah,   ah.) _____   Come on,   Dave, _   play   it   for   me   now!

3↘ 3↑   4↘   4↓

Outro-Harmonica Solo

Am   Dm7

Yeah!

6↓ 6↑ 5↓ 4↓ 4↘ 4↓   6↓ 6↑ 6↓ 7↑ 8↓ 9↓ 9↑ 9↓ 8↓   7↑   7↓ 8↓ 7↓ 6↓ 6↑   5↓ 4↓

Am

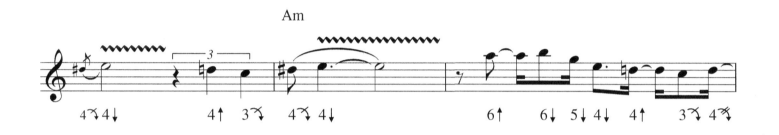

4↘ 4↓   4↑ 3↘ 4↘ 4↓   6↑   6↓ 5↓ 4↓ 4↑ 3↘ 4↘

Dm7   Am

3↘ 3↑   (3↑)   4↑ 4↘ (4↘)   (4↘)

Begin fade
Dm7   Am

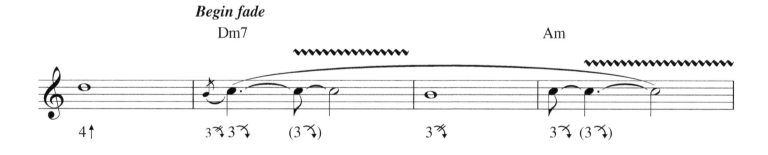

4↑   3↘ 3↘ (3↘)   3↘   3↘ (3↘)

Fade out

Dm7

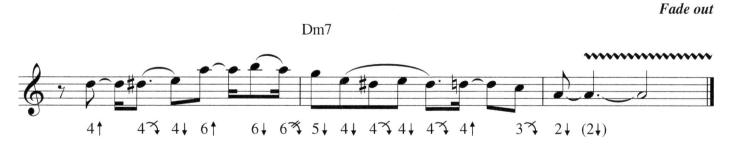

4↑   4↘ 4↓ 6↑   6↓ 6↘ 5↓ 4↓ 4↘ 4↓ 4↘ 4↑   3↘ 2↓ (2↓)

Take the Long Way Home

HARMONICA

Player: Rick Davies
Harp Key: F Diatonic

Words and Music by Rick Davies and Roger Hodgson

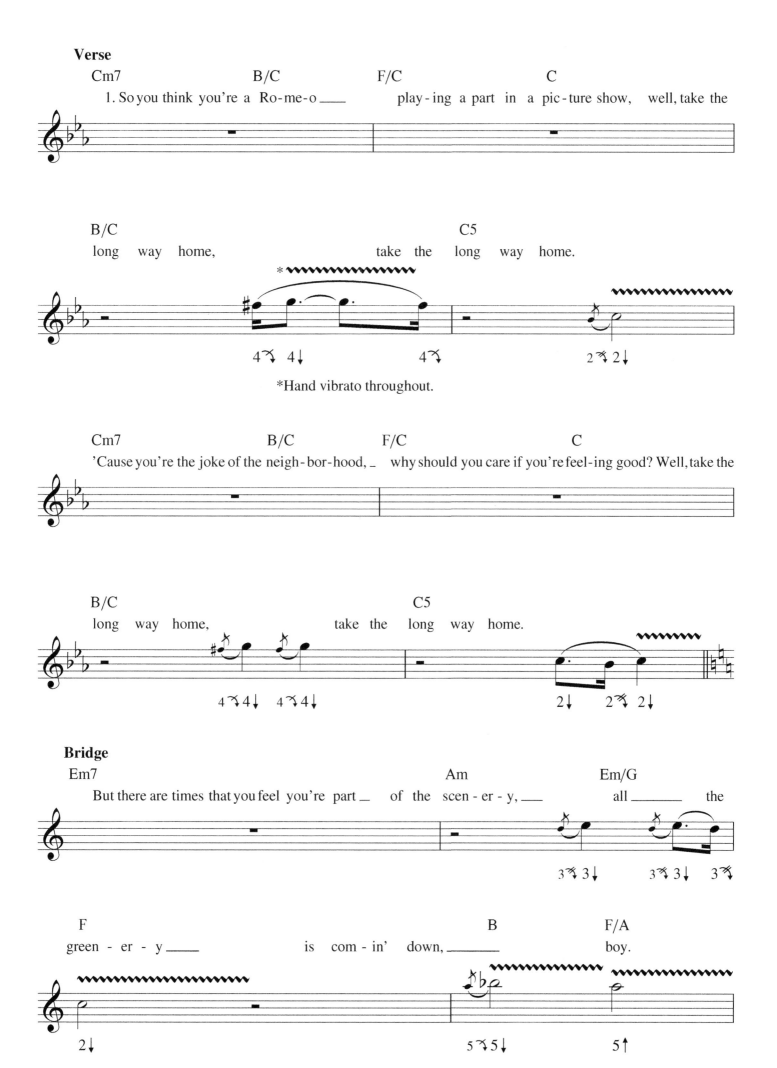

Verse

Cm7   B/C   F/C   C

1. So you think you're a Ro-me-o ⎯⎯ play-ing a part in a pic-ture show, well, take the

B/C   C5

long   way   home,   take   the   long   way   home.

*Hand vibrato throughout.

Cm7   B/C   F/C   C

'Cause you're the joke of the neigh-bor-hood, ⎯ why should you care if you're feel-ing good? Well, take the

B/C   C5

long   way   home,   take   the   long   way   home.

Bridge

Em7   Am   Em/G

But there are times that you feel you're part ⎯ of the scen-er-y, ⎯ all ⎯⎯⎯ the

F   B   F/A

green - er - y ⎯⎯ is com - in' down, ⎯⎯⎯ boy.

*Played as straight sixteenth-notes.

*Played as even sixteenth-notes.

Interlude

Outro

Free time

Additional Lyrics

Does it feel that your life's become a catastrophe?
Oh, it has to be for you to grow, boy.
When you look through the years and see what you could have been,
Oh, what you might have been, if you'd had more time.

HARMONICA NOTATION LEGEND

Harmonica music can be notated two different ways: on a *musical staff*, and in *tablature*.

THE MUSICAL STAFF shows pitches and rhythms and is divided by bar lines into measures. Pitches are named after the first seven letters of the alphabet.

TABLATURE graphically represents the harmonica music. Each note will be accompanied by a number, 1 through 10, indicating what hole you are to play. The arrow that follows indicates whether to blow or draw. (All examples are shown using a C diatonic harmonica.)

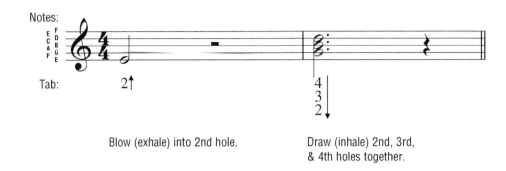

Blow (exhale) into 2nd hole.

Draw (inhale) 2nd, 3rd, & 4th holes together.

Notes on the C Harmonica

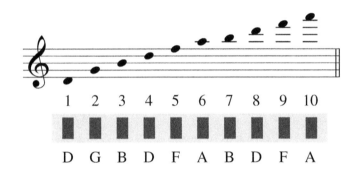

Exhaled (Blown) Notes

1	2	3	4	5	6	7	8	9	10
C	E	G	C	E	G	C	E	G	C

Inhaled (Drawn) Notes

1	2	3	4	5	6	7	8	9	10
D	G	B	D	F	A	B	D	F	A

Bends

Blow Bends

- 1/4 step
- 1/2 step
- 1 step
- 1 1/2 steps

Draw Bends

- 1/4 step
- 1/2 step
- 1 step
- 1 1/2 steps

Definitions for Special Harmonica Notation

SLURRED BEND: Play (draw) 3rd hole, then bend the note down one whole step.

3↓　3↘

GRACE NOTE BEND: Starting with a pre-bent note, immediately release bend to the target note.

2↘ 2↓

VIBRATO: Begin adding vibrato to the sustained note on beat 3.

4↑　(4↑)

TONGUE BLOCKING: Using your tongue to block holes 2 & 3, play octaves on holes 1 & 4.

4↑
1

NOTE: Tablature numbers in parentheses are used when:

- The note is sustained, but a new articulation begins (such as vibrato), or
- The quantity of notes being sustained changes, or
- A change in dynamics (volume) occurs.

Additional Musical Definitions

D.S. al Coda

- Go back to the sign (𝄋), then play until the measure marked "***To Coda***," then skip to the section labelled "**Coda**."

D.C. al Fine

- Go back to the beginning of the song and play until the measure marked "***Fine***" (end).

- Repeat measures between signs.

(accent)

- Accentuate the note (play initial attack louder).

(staccato)

- Play the note short.

- When a repeated section has different endings, play the first ending only the first time and the second ending only the second time.

Dynamics

p

- Piano (soft)

mp

- Mezzo Piano (medium soft)

mf

- Mezzo Forte (medium loud)

f

- Forte (loud)

(crescendo)

- Gradually louder

(decrescendo)

- Gradually softer

HAL•LEONARD® HARMONICA PLAY-ALONG

Play your favorite songs quickly and easily!

Just follow the notation, listen to the audio to hear how the harmonica should sound, and then play along using the separate full-band backing tracks. The melody and lyrics are also included in the book in case you want to sing, or to simply help you follow along. The audio includes playback tools so you can adjust the recording to any tempo without changing pitch!

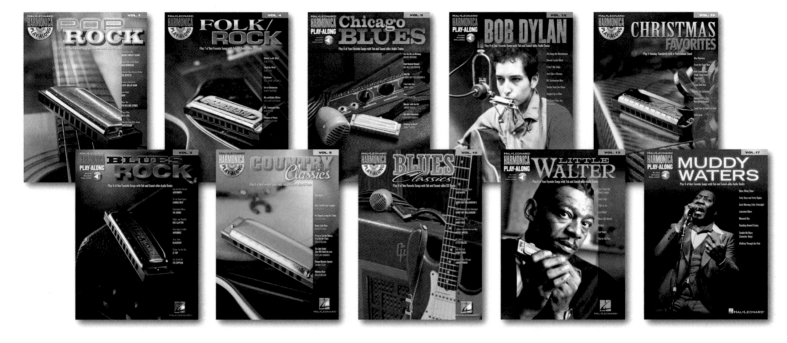

1. Pop/Rock
And When I Die • Bright Side of the Road • I Should Have Known Better • Low Rider • Miss You • Piano Man • Take the Long Way Home • You Don't Know How It Feels.
00000478 Book/CD Pack $16.99

2. Rock Hits
Cowboy • Hand in My Pocket • Karma Chameleon • Middle of the Road • Run Around • Smokin' in the Boys Room • Train in Vain • What I like About You.
00000479 Book/CD Pack $14.99

3. Blues/Rock
Big Ten Inch Record • On the Road Again • Road-house Blues • Rollin' and Tumblin' • Train Kept A-Rollin' • Train, Train • Waitin' for the Bus • You Shook Me.
00000481 Book/Online Audio $15.99

4. Folk/Rock
Blowin' in the Wind • Catch the Wind • Daydream • Eve of Destruction • Me and Bobby McGee • Mr. Tambourine Man • Pastures of Plenty.
00000482 Book/CD Pack $14.99

5. Country Classics
Blue Bayou • Don't Tell Me Your Troubles • He Stopped Loving Her Today • Honky Tonk Blues • If You've Got the Money (I've Got the Time) • The Only Daddy That Will Walk the Line • Orange Blossom Special • Whiskey River.
00001004 Book/CD Pack $14.99

6. Country Hits
Ain't Goin' down ('Til the Sun Comes Up) • Drive (For Daddy Gene) • Getcha Some • Here's a Quarter (Call Someone Who Cares) • Honkytonk U • One More Last Chance • Put Yourself in My Shoes • Turn It Loose.
00001013 Book/CD Pack $14.99

8. Pop Classics
Bluesette • Cherry Pink and Apple Blossom White • From Me to You • Love Me Do • Midnight Cowboy • Moon River • Peg O' My Heart • A Rainy Night in Georgia.
00001090 Book/Online Audio $14.99

9. Chicago Blues
Blues with a Feeling • Easy • Got My Mo Jo Working • Help Me • I Ain't Got You • Juke • Messin' with the Kid.
00001091 Book/Online Audio..................$15.99

10. Blues Classics
Baby, Scratch My Back • Eyesight to the Blind • Good Morning Little Schoolgirl • Honest I Do • I'm Your Hoochie Coochie Man • My Babe • Ride and Roll • Sweet Home Chicago.
00001093 Book/CD Pack $15.99

11. Christmas Carols
Angels We Have Heard on High • Away in a Manger • Deck the Hall • The First Noel • Go, Tell It on the Mountain • Jingle Bells • Joy to the World • O Little Town of Bethlehem.
00001296 Book/CD Pack $12.99

12. Bob Dylan
All Along the Watchtower • Blowin' in the Wind • It Ain't Me Babe • Just like a Woman • Mr. Tambourine Man • Shelter from the Storm • Tangled up in Blue • The Times They Are A-Changin'.
00001326 Book/Online Audio..................$16.99

13. Little Walter
Can't Hold Out Much Longer • Crazy Legs • I Got to Go • Last Night • Mean Old World • Rocker • Sad Hours • You're So Fine.
00001334 Book/Online Audio $14.99

14. Jazz Standards
Autumn Leaves • Georgia on My Mind • Lullaby of Birdland • Meditation (Meditacao) • My Funny Valentine • Satin Doll • Some Day My Prince Will Come • What a Wonderful World.
00001335 Book/CD Pack $16.99

15. Jazz Classics
All Blues • Au Privave • Comin' Home Baby • Song for My Father • Sugar • Sunny • Take Five • Work Song.
00001336 Book/CD Pack $14.99

16. Christmas Favorites
Blue Christmas • Frosty the Snow Man • Here Comes Santa Claus (Right down Santa Claus Lane) • Jingle-Bell Rock • Nuttin' for Christmas • Rudolph the Red-Nosed Reindeer • Santa Claus Is Comin' to Town • Silver Bells.
00001350 Book/CD Pack $14.99

17. Muddy Waters
Blow, Wind, Blow • Forty Days and Forty Nights • Good Morning Little Schoolgirl • Louisiana Blues • Mannish Boy • Standing Around Crying • Trouble No More (Someday Baby) • Walking Through the Park.
00821043 Book/Online Audio.................$14.99

HAL•LEONARD®
Order online from your favorite music retailer
at **www.halleonard.com**

Prices, content, and availability subject to change without notice.

0820
432

THE HAL LEONARD HARMONICA METHOD AND SONGBOOKS

THE METHOD

THE HAL LEONARD COMPLETE HARMONICA METHOD — CHROMATIC HARMONICA
by Bobby Joe Holman

The only harmonica method to present the chromatic harmonica in 14 scales and modes in all 12 keys! This book will take beginners from the basics on through to the most advanced techniques available for the contemporary harmonica player. Each section contains appropriate songs and exercises that enable the player to quickly learn the various concepts presented. Every aspect of this versatile musical instrument is explored and explained in easy-to-understand detail with illustrations. The musical styles covered include traditional, blues, pop and rock.

00841286 Book/Online Audio.............................. $12.99

THE HAL LEONARD COMPLETE HARMONICA METHOD — DIATONIC HARMONICA
by Bobby Joe Holman

The only harmonica method specific to the diatonic harmonica, covering all six positions. This book/audio pack contains over 20 songs and musical examples that take beginners from the basics on through to the most advanced techniques available for the contemporary harmonica player. Each section contains appropriate songs and exercises (which are demonstrated through the online video) that enable the player to quickly learn the various concepts presented. Every aspect of this versatile musical instrument is explored and explained in easy-to-understand detail with illustrations. The musical styles covered include traditional, blues, pop and rock.

00841285 Book/Online Audio.............................. $12.99

THE SONGBOOKS

The Hal Leonard Harmonica Songbook series offers a wide variety of music especially tailored to the two-volume Hal Leonard Harmonica Method, but can be played by all harmonica players, diatonic and chromatic alike. All books include study and performance notes, and a guide to harmonica tablature. From classical themes to Christmas music, rock and roll to Broadway, there's something for everyone!

BROADWAY SONGS FOR HARMONICA
arranged by Bobby Joe Holman

19 show-stopping Broadway tunes for the harmonica. Songs include: Ain't Misbehavin' • Bali Ha'i • Camelot • Climb Ev'ry Mountain • Do-Re-Mi • Edelweiss • Give My Regards to Broadway • Hello, Dolly! • I've Grown Accustomed to Her Face • The Impossible Dream (The Quest) • Memory • Oklahoma • People • and more.
00820009 .... $9.95

CLASSICAL FAVORITES FOR HARMONICA
arranged by Bobby Joe Holman

18 famous classical melodies and themes, arranged for diatonic and chromatic players. Includes: By the Beautiful Blue Danube • Clair De Lune • The Flight of the Bumble Bee • Gypsy Rondo • Moonlight Sonata • Surprise Symphony • The Swan (Le Cygne) • Waltz of the Flowers • and more, plus a guide to harmonica tablature.
00820006 .... $10.99

MOVIE FAVORITES FOR HARMONICA
arranged by Bobby Joe Holman

19 songs from the silver screen, arranged for diatonic and chromatic harmonica. Includes: Alfie • Bless the Beasts and Children • Chim Chim Cher-ee • The Entertainer • Georgy Girl • Midnight Cowboy • Moon River • Picnic • Speak Softly, Love • Stormy Weather • Tenderly • Unchained Melody • What a Wonderful World • and more, plus a guide to harmonica tablature.
00820014 .... $9.95

HAL•LEONARD®

Visit Hal Leonard Online at
www.halleonard.com